Drawing Turtles
How to Draw Turtles
For the Beginner

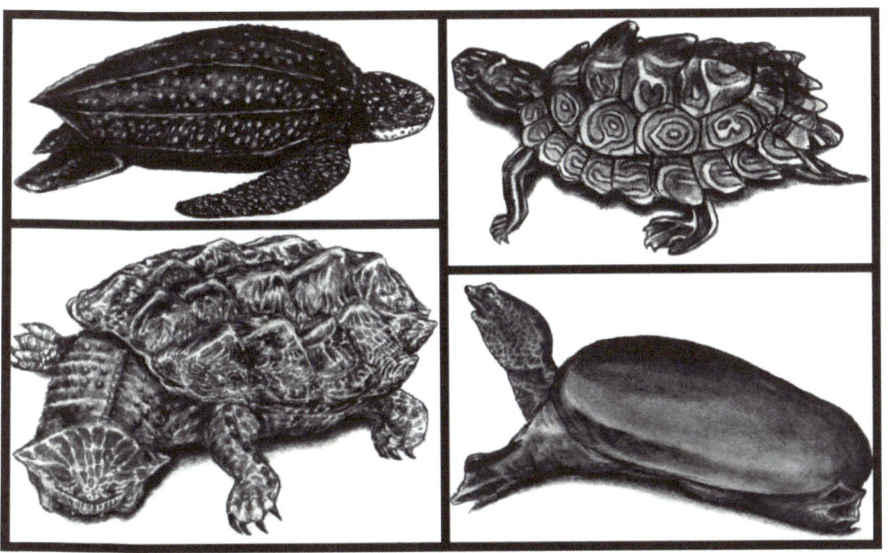

Learn to Draw Series
Adrian Sanqui

Mendon Cottage Books

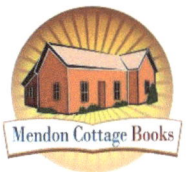

JD-Biz Publishing

Learn How to Draw Books for the Absolute Beginner

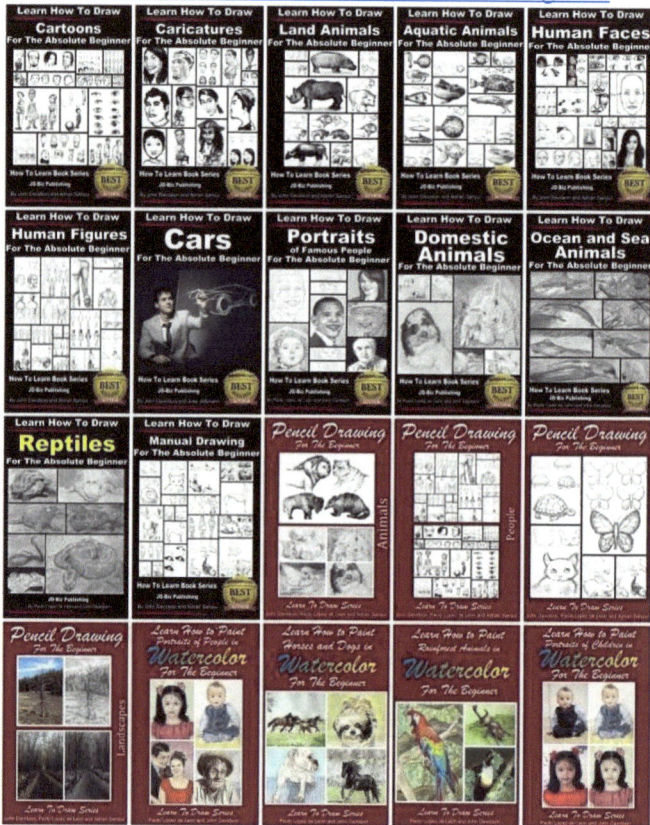

Table of Contents

Drawing tools

Pencils

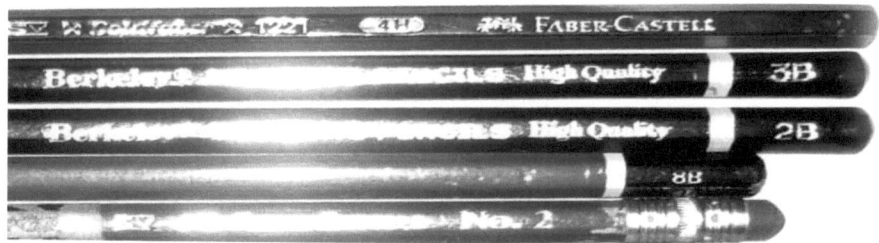

The most important tool you need to be able to enhance your drawing skills is a medium that can be corrected if you made some sloppy line strokes. Knowing and using more than just one type of pencil is a big help and it is better if you have pencils of different grades so you can easily produce the kind of lightness or darkness you want to make. The 'H' engraved near the pencil's tip (side of eraser) stands for "hardness" and it ranges from 2H to 9H. A pencil with only an "H" mark and doesn't have a number means 1H. The most common type (the one available anywhere) of pencil that does not indicate its grade mark is usually a 2H pencil. The "B" marking of pencils stand for "blackness", this means that they can easily produce darker line marks and are softer than H pencils. It ranges from HB (hard and dark) to 9B (very soft and very dark), so when it comes to B pencils, the higher the number is; the softer and darker it becomes. Different brands have different softness, hardness and blackness levels, so if you are going to use a certain brand for the first time, you should try them out first before applying it on your main drawing.

Charcoal pencils

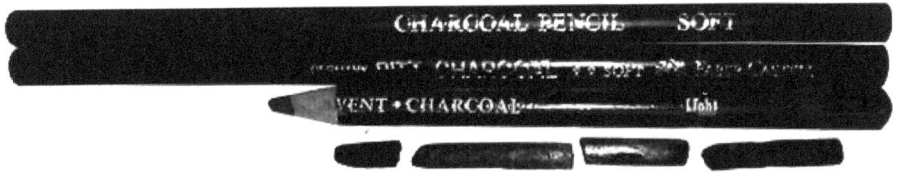

Charcoal pencils also come in different grades. The generic grades of soft, medium and hard are available in different brands. Charcoal pencils are a bit messy to work with; even the 'hard' grade charcoal pencil is still relatively softer compared to those with 4B to 6B grade pencils. It is most advisable for drawings that would require a lot of smeared shading for a smoother and wider portrayal of gradation.

Mechanical pencil

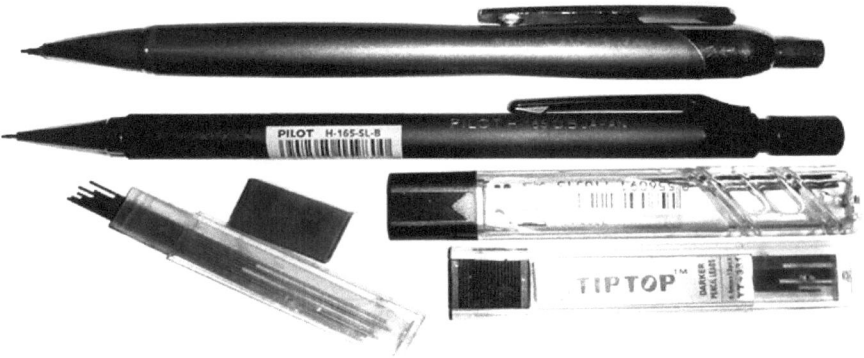

A mechanical pencil has a consistent wick or point which makes it easier for you to maintain the thickness of the line marks you produce. Mechanical pencils are good for small and subtle detailing that requires very thin lines, instead of sharpening your pencil several times just to have a thin and constant fine point that you need. Different grades of lead or graphite is also available for refilling your mechanical pencil, just make sure that the size of the point your pencil has is also the same as the pencil leads you refill it with. They come in several sizes and style, but what really matters is it does what it's supposed to.

Sharpener

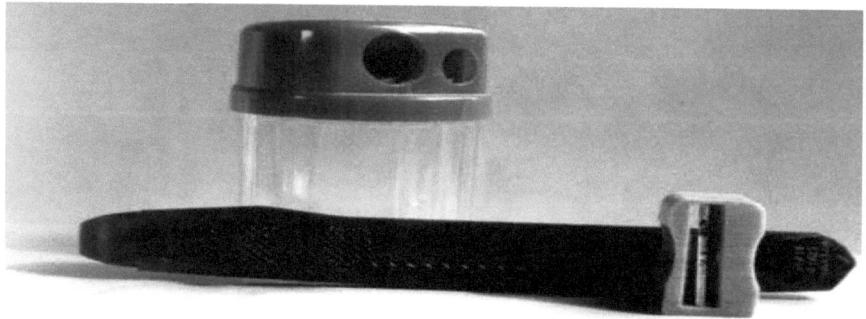

A regular sharpener is quite dependable if you are using H and low B pencils, but if you are going to use it to sharpen a pencil with very soft graphite cores then it may keep on breaking, most especially if you will use it for a charcoal lead pencil. A good substitute for regular sharpeners is a cutter, so you can easily control the pressure that should just be enough to expose the core and achieve a fine point. Cutters are often used if you want a "chisel" point pencil that is very helpful for thick and thin linings.

Erasers

Pencils are no good if you don't have a good quality eraser, having an eraser is essential if you are going to use a pencil for drawing. Choose a rubber

---

eraser that is soft and not the ones that leave a faint color or worst is a scratch on the paper.

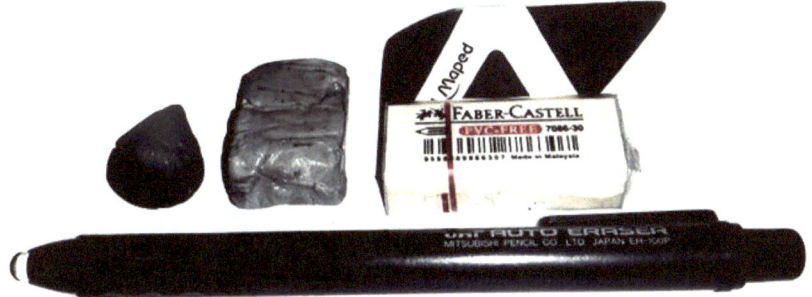

Don't leave your eraser lying around on the table or just anywhere, keep it on a pencil case or anything that can protect it from being exposed on air for too long because some erasers (cheaper ones) harden when it's left lying around because it will dry out and harden.

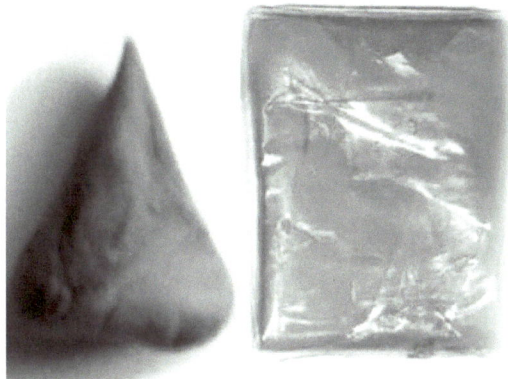

A kneadable eraser is very helpful for making highlights and reaching hardly accessible areas such as the gloss on the eyes or light portions of fingernails and such. It usually looks like a gray slab or a small bar of clay that can be molded or deformed to any shape you desire. It doesn't rub off the marking like usual erasers, but instead, it lifts off the graphite from the paper, like absorbing it. Instead of rubbing the eraser with a certain pressure to remove a marking, carefully dab on the portions you want to erase or to simply decrease the applied graphite or charcoal until you recover the brightness (whiteness of the paper) you want. Kneaded erasers can still be useful as long as they aren't already too dirty or dry. Keep it in a concealed container to lengthen its usefulness, because just like how good it is for absorbing graphite, it would also easily catch dust.

Smudge sticks

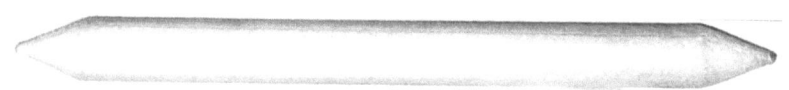

A smudge stick is used for smearing the shades on the portions that are hard to access. Some artists dull down the other tip so it can be used for distributing the shades on the big areas. To avoid ruining the smudge stick, use a sand paper to make a blunter tip or to make it even pointier. Smudge sticks or blending stumps comes in different sizes, choose what best fits your needs and it will be a big help for blending gradations. Smudge sticks are cheap and are available on art stores. Common smudge sticks are just rolled and compressed hard papers, so try not to get it wet.

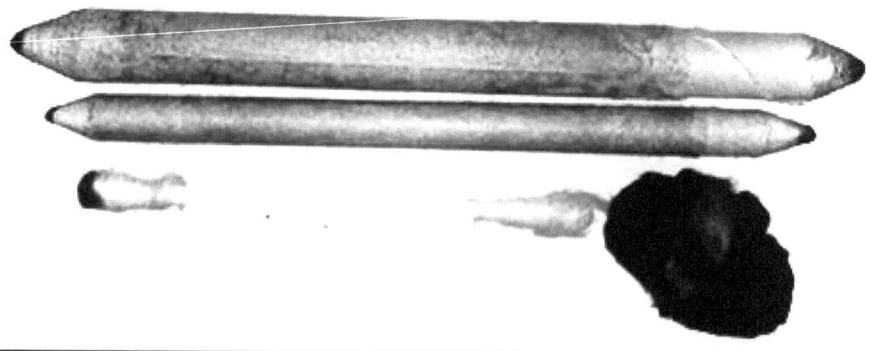

Keep those used up smudge sticks even if it's already in a rugged state (dirty or worn out), you never know when it might get handy. Dirty smudge sticks are useful for producing faint shades, and those with torn up tips can make textures that you might find useful.

If ever you cannot find a smudge stick available (although, I doubt this would be a problem if you have art stores near you, and if not, you can just order online. It is quite cheap) you can just make a tortillion for a temporary smudging tool (some artists actually prefer this one instead of smudge sticks). Use a thick piece of paper (like those on sketch pads, preferably the ones for watercolor drawings. Do not use thin and shiny papers). Fold it on one side and roll it up to create a cone, with the folded side at the tip.

Coloring materials

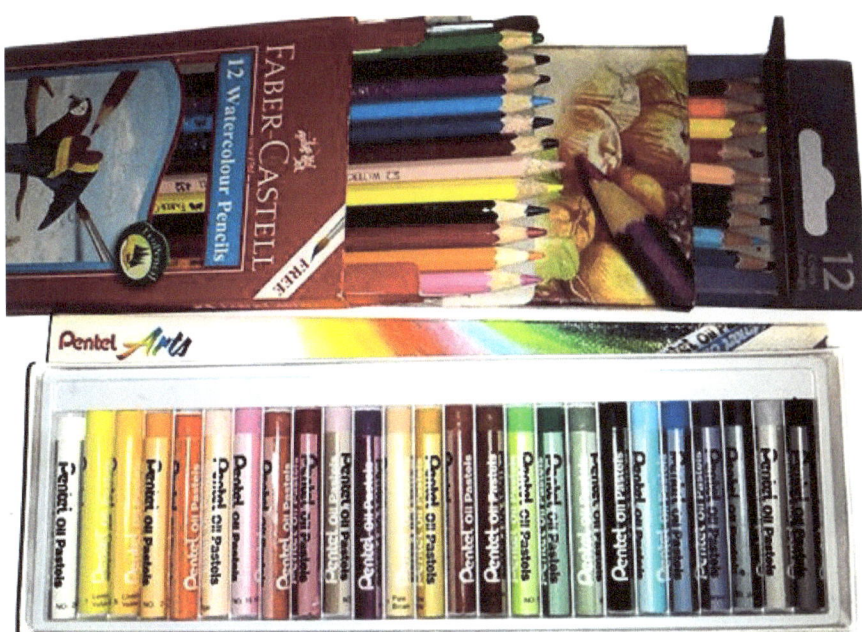

If you are planning to color your drawing, choose a coloring tool that best fits your needs.

Oil pastels are good for blending and synchronizing different colors together. It might get messy on your first trials (if you don't want to get messy, just place a clean piece of paper for your palm rest, to avoid rubbing your palm against the colored portions of your drawing) but you'll get the hang of it as you use it more often. Oil pastels are good for beginners as a practicing tool for smearing different color values.

Color pencils are the next best thing for filling your drawing with colored hatches (linear shading), or even coloring via scribbling. This coloring tool is best for small-sized illustrations. Although, the peak of the tone values that a common color pencil set can produce are far weaker than the oil pastel's, and it cannot be smeared (but there are available color pencils which can produce strong color tones just like oil pastel's or even acrylic's, but they are quite pricy; like the prisma color pencils). This coloring tool is also a good practicing medium for beginners, and my personal favorite for quick colored sketches or even for illustrations with fairly detailed line work.

Parts of a Turtle

It is better of you are familiar with the basic parts of a turtle if you are going to draw one (instead of guessing about the specifics, such as the number and order of the shell's scales). You can use the image below to recognize the parts of a common turtle so you could properly construct the figure. But you should know that not all the turtles have the same form; it is given that all have the same number of limbs, eyes and such, but take note that other turtles have different set of scutes, placements and sizes of facial features, and body length.

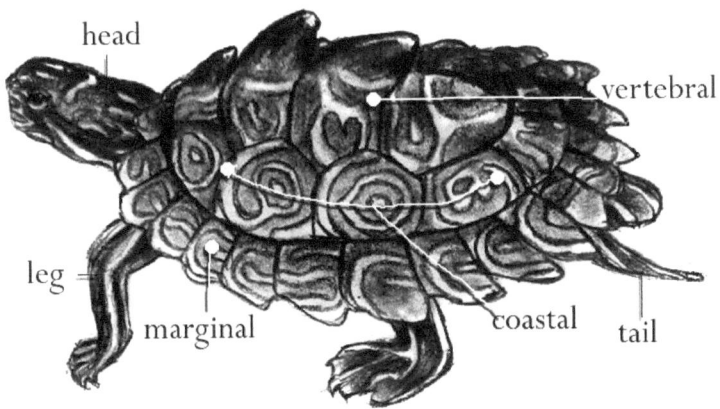

Most turtles have a reasonably long neck so they can reach their food, since they cannot position their body vertically. The head shape is usually common to a reptile's, an oval shape that has more mass on the portion connected to the neck. Most turtles that often surface the ground have nails, which help them hold down their food and to have a better grip of the ground when they crawl. The eyes are often positioned on the side (but there are few who have eyes that are set on the upper corners of the head).

The shell of a turtle is divided into two major parts; the carapace, which is the dorsal/upper side, and the plastron, which is underside/ventral.

The carapace is made of thick plates or scales called scutes, and the row of scales are identified according to their placement. The smaller scales at the edges of the carapace are the marginal scutes. The nuchal scute is the first large plate positioned on the subsiding area of the shell following the cervical scale above the turtle's nape, and the utmost top of the shell which is the middle row following the nuchal scale (three scales that are often the widest ones) covering the spine of the turtle are the vertebral plates/scales. And the last plate of the middle row in-between the last vertebral scale and the pygal shield (the scale above the tail) is the suprapygal scale. The rows in-between the vertebral scales and the marginal scales are called the costal scutes (eight scales, four in each row, that are usually smaller than the vertebral scales).

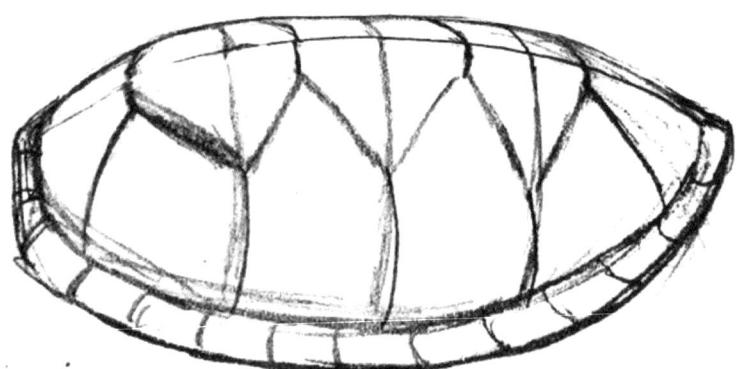

A certain pattern of reference line marks can be used to easily establish the scutes of a turtle's shell. Just simply curve this lines with the dimension of the shell no matter what kind of shape it can be compared to or degree of convexity it has.

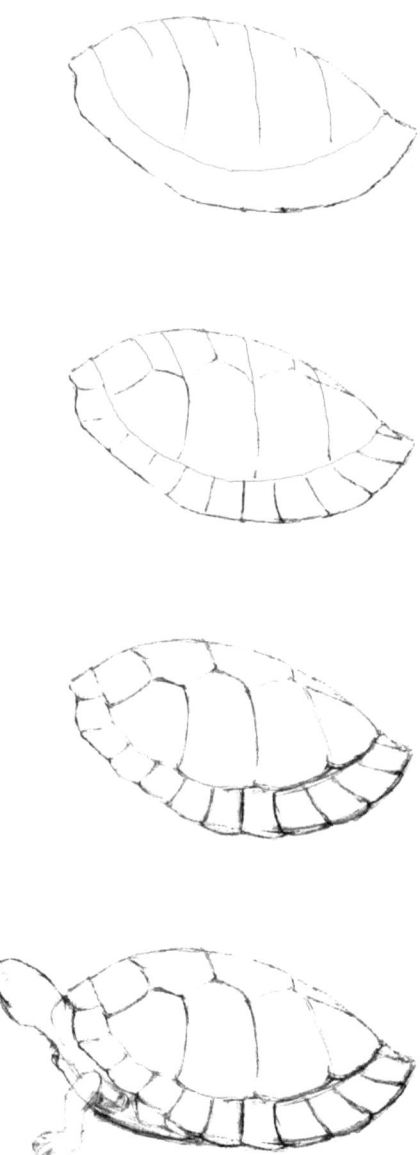

How to Draw the Shell of a Turtle Easily

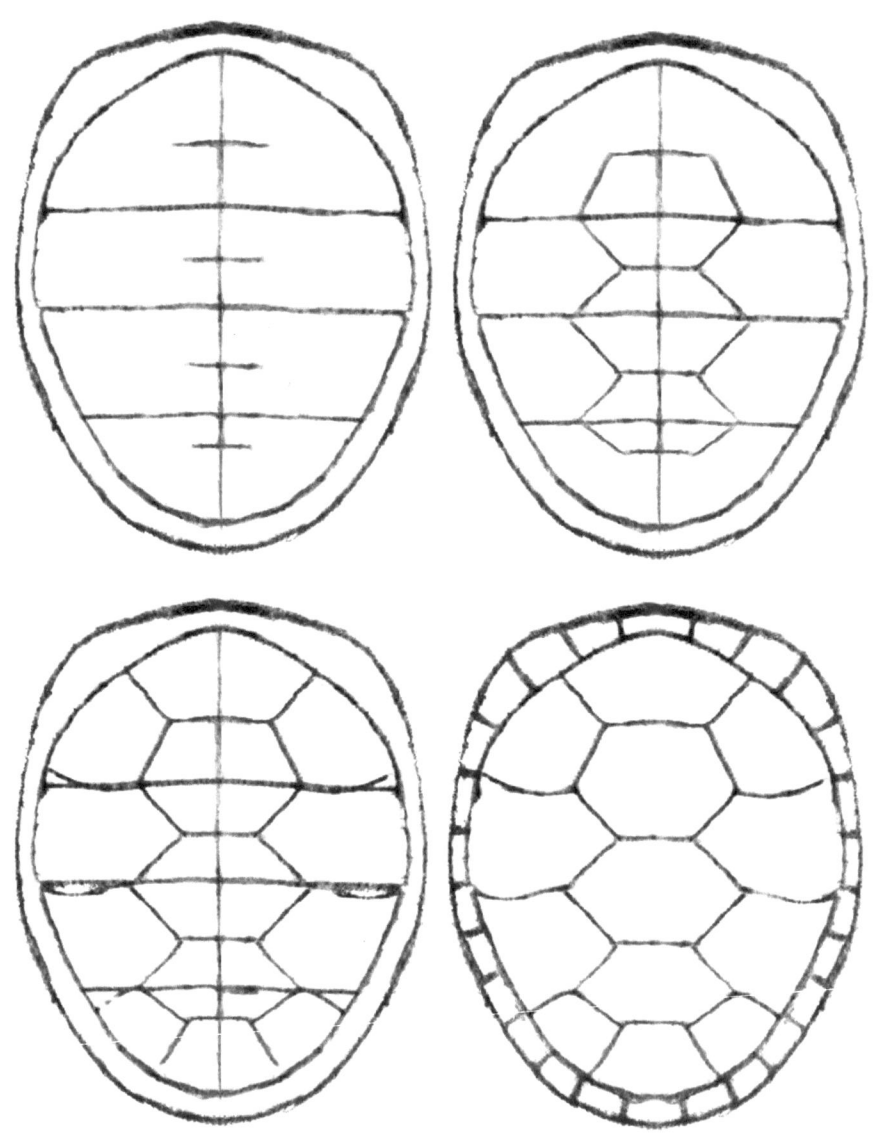

Different Types of Turtle Shells

The shapes of the turtles' carapaces vary in different forms and size. Aside from the basic shape structure, some turtle shells contain unique features like spikes or knobs with a certain number and position depending on the turtle species. The texture of the shell's surface also varies; some have a fairly smooth texture and some are rough (having a number of ridges or protuberances).

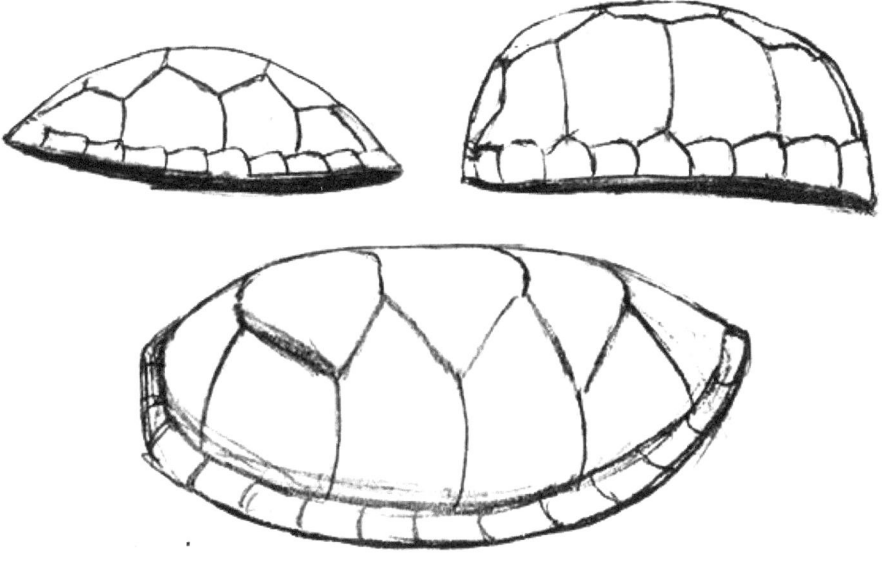

The most common form is the bowl-shaped shell that is often seen on land turtles. The height and thickness of the bowl-shaped carapaces are also used as an identifier for several turtle species; such as the box turtle (named before its robust and almost box-shaped carapace that looks more like a hard helmet than a soup bowl). The margining edges of the shells also differ in its manner of slope and evenness. Some shells have smooth curvy outlines while others are almost straight. There are certain types of turtles that are noted for their unique shell margins, such as the knobbed sawback turtle that has a shell with toothed edges.

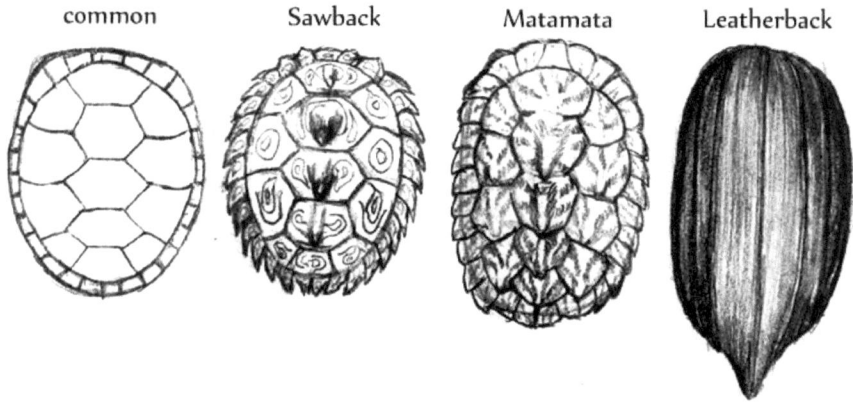

common   Sawback   Matamata   Leatherback

Not all turtle shells are hard-plated or formed with scutes. There are turtles that are noted for their really unique carapaces. Most of them are marine types and few on land turtle species; like the softshell turtle, having a shell that is relatively flat (like a pancake covering its body), or the leatherback sea turtle that has an elongated tear-shaped leathery carapace.

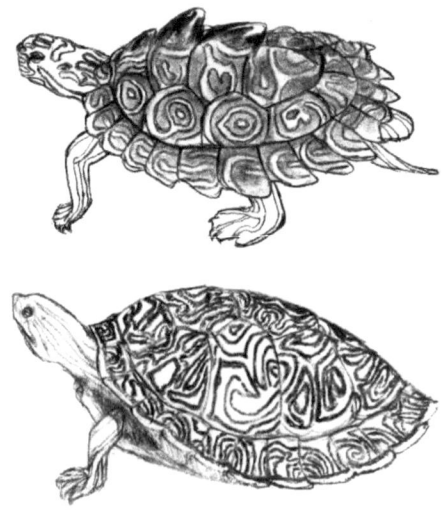

The markings on a turtle's shell also differ depending on its kind. The prints on each scale of map turtles are often like swirls of rings with thick outlines, the eastern box turtle's carapace are like random inkblots, while the markings on the shell of a river cooter are several layers of random line patterns like maze puzzle outlines.

Black-knobbed Map Turtle

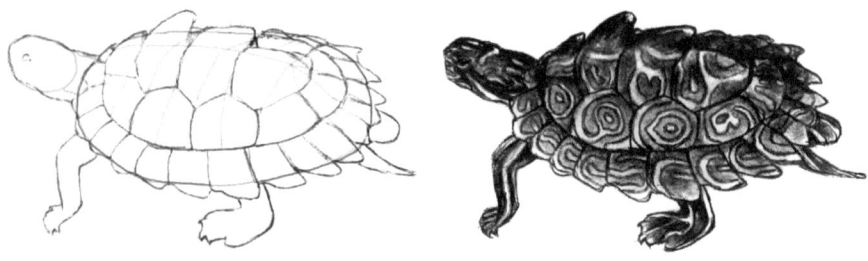

The black knobbed map turtle or the black-knobbed sawback (scientifically referred to as Graptemus nigrinoda), as name/s suggest, has a row of protuberances or knobs spiking out from its carapace. It inhabits active streams and rivers with fresh water (it cannot live on salt water systems).

This turtle is native to southeast of United States; in Mississippi and Alabama, swimming the fresh water streams of Black Warrior River and Tombigbee, and along the high north of Jefferson County. The females are relatively bigger than the males; growing a shell length of five to seven inches, (mature males can only grow a shell length of three to four inches).

The coloration of a black-knobbed turtle is basically green to brown. The skin (head and limbs) is usually green (Either dark or light green), containing thin pale-yellow to off-white linings and green stripes of a different tone value. The carapace is either green or faint-brown, the shape is basically oval with toothed/saw-like edges. Each plate or scale of the shell contains ring patterns, the ring prints could either be pale-yellow or green of a brighter value, outlined with black or faint-brown (on a dark green surface). The four scales at middle row covering the spinal column (row of the vertebral plate) of the turtle have pointed protrusions each, spiking rearward. These spiking knobs are often black or black-tipped, and always differ in size; the first one is quite short compared to the second and third knob (the third knob being the longest spike) and the fourth one is barely protruding (more like a fold or a slope on the scute rather than a spike).

- Create the base form of the turtle to easily establish its figure. Simply define the shape of the shell and the size of the head using ovals. Angle the figure according to your liking and properly adjust the shapes if necessary.

- Use the reference lines to define the scutes properly.
Define the inner edges by establishing the marginal shells. And then place the reference guides to convey the proper division and placement of each scute.

Define the scute with the help of the reference lines you placed. Make any adjustments to their size, shape and position if necessary. Make sure that the scutes are properly angled with the position of your turtle (in this case, upper side view).

- Add the features outside the base (oval).
Based on the established marginal scutes, add the saw-like edges of each one. Each saw-like spikes should point rearward (with the middle scute above the area of the tail having a triangular edge pointing straight).

And the limbs and the tail. Take note that in this angle, the farther legs are hidden (with the foreleg being completely unseen and the hind leg being overlapped by the base).

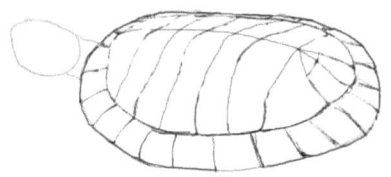

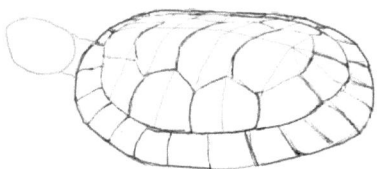

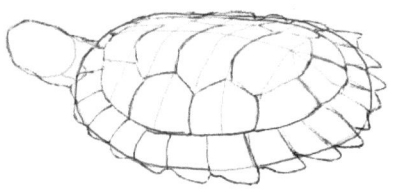

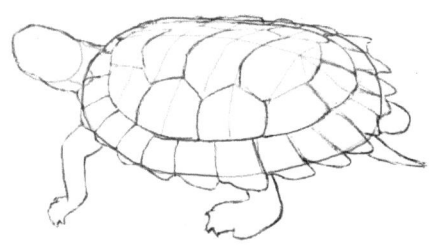

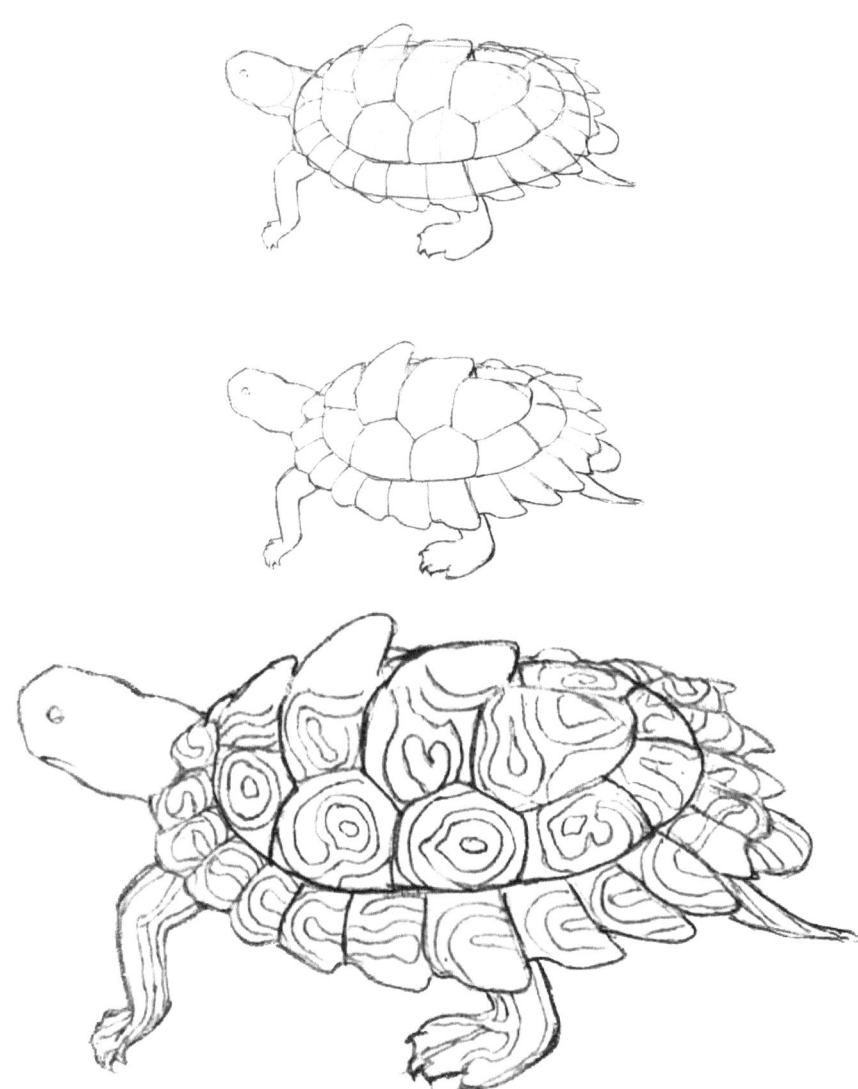

- Define the knobs on the shell.

Use the horizontal reference line to properly apply the unique feature of the black-knobbed turtle, with the first knob being the smallest visible spike and the second as the longest one. The fourth protuberance should only appear like a fold on the convex of the fourth vertebral scale.

- Clean up the drawing.

Erase the reference lines when all the necessary outlines of the turtle's form are established.

- Convey the markings of the body and the shell.

Draw the details of the shell. Establish the random swirly outlines inside the scutes and stripe marks on the turtle's skin. The marking on the shell are better portrayed individually (different swirl per scute, including the marginal shells), these prints are not patterned to flow continuously (lines not connecting to the other lines).

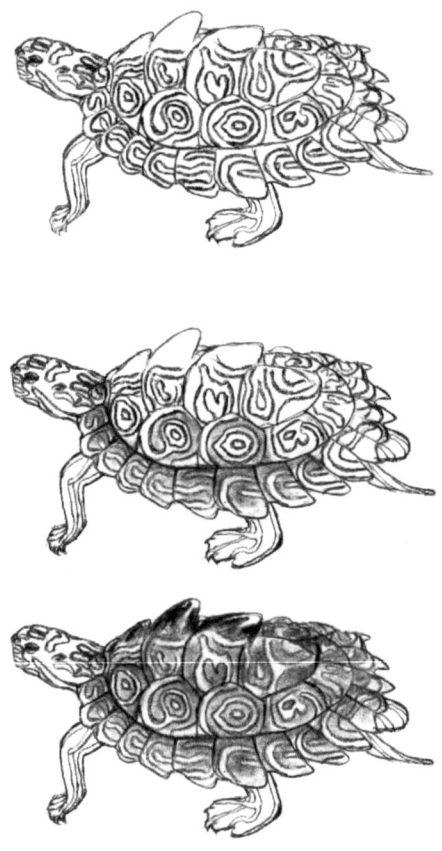

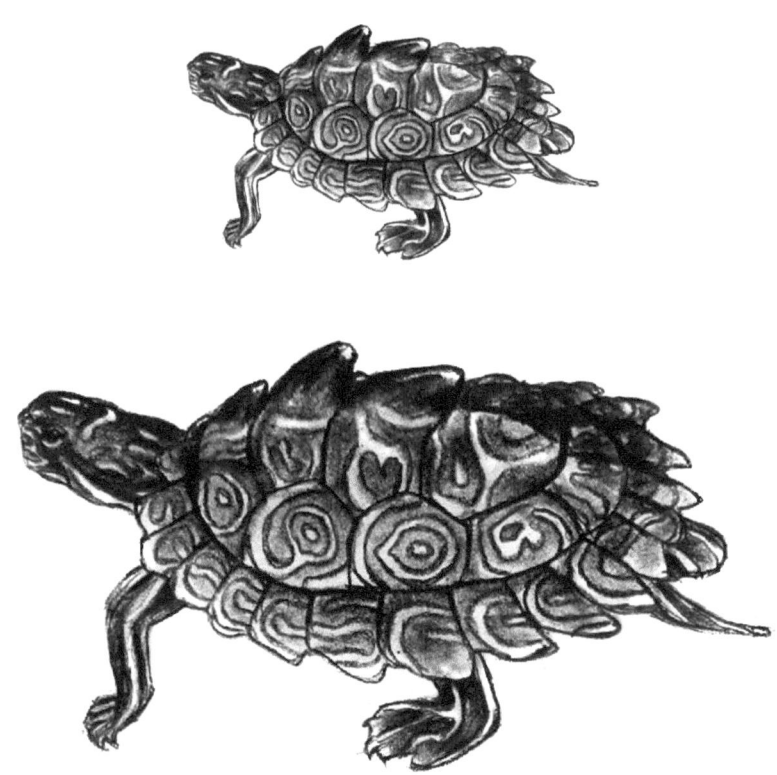

- Thicken the outline of the swirls.

Re-define the outline of the markings using a blunt-point or the side of the pencil.

- Shade the areas outside of the swirls.

The swirls should have a brighter value. Apply some shades at the portions outside of the swirls of each scale/scute.

Darken the knobs (they should be black). Leave some highlights on each black knobs to portray its mass and semi-glossy texture.

- Darken the tone value.

Apply the dark skin tone of the turtle (the linings should be avoided since they have bright values) and redefine the gradation entirely. The darkest areas of the turtle should be the black knobs and the farther side of the head, while the second/middle tone should be the scutes excluding the prints, and the brightest parts should be the prints (swirls and stripes).

- Re-darken the farther side of the shell.

The farther side of the shell should appear darker than the nearer side to further establish the position and angle of the turtle.

Cast the shadow of the figure and clean up the drawing. Redefine the main outlines if necessary.

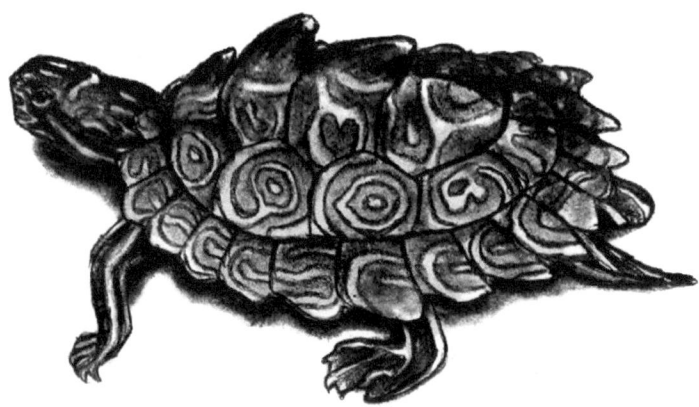

This turtle loves the heat of the sun, it can be seen basking on top of floating logs or on rocks surfacing above the water, but it is shy and cautious when it is above water surface: it would quickly jump on the water if it senses any threat because they can move faster on water than on land.

Leatherback Sea Turtle

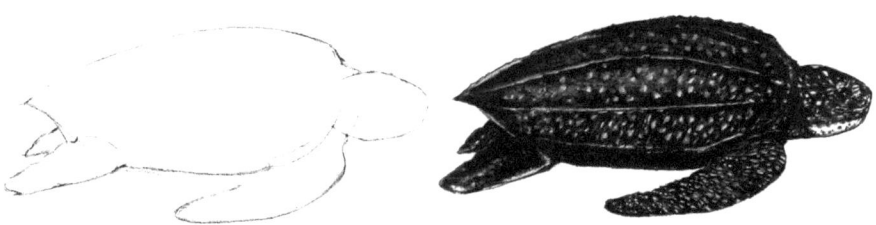

Known as the biggest amongst any other, this turtle can grow a length of approximately six to nine feet, having a carapace length of four to seven feet. It is unique and very rare to see. Aside from its huge size, it is the only remaining member of its kind.

Its primary diet is jellyfish and other soft tissues marine creatures; it would travel for a long period of time searching for food, swimming the vast ocean of significant distance to search for a location to hunt.

Apparently, they often mistakenly recognize floating plastic wastes for a jellyfish. An alarming number of leatherback sea turtles' deaths were due to ingesting plastic bags; as a native traveler of the seas, it would come across an urbanized area where plastics are carelessly disposed frequently.

As the name suggests, the leather back sea turtle has a long and unique carapace. It has a bean-shaped (tear-shaped) shell and has a texture that can be compared to a leather, having seven protuberant linings dorsally. Its oval head is bulky and relatively big, so as the limbs. As a sea turtle, the limbs are flattened so it could move/swim with ease on its habitat (it is actually the fastest swimming reptile according to Guinness world record).

The front flippers are large and wide (larger than any other of its kind) when folded on the side, the length of its front flippers are more than the half of its shell length. The rear flippers are at least half or less of the front flippers' length. Its body color is dark; from dark gray to faint black, having white spotting all around its body (head, flippers and carapace), mostly on the flippers and the lower areas of the head. The underside of its body has a lighter color value; from pinkish- white to off/grayish-white.

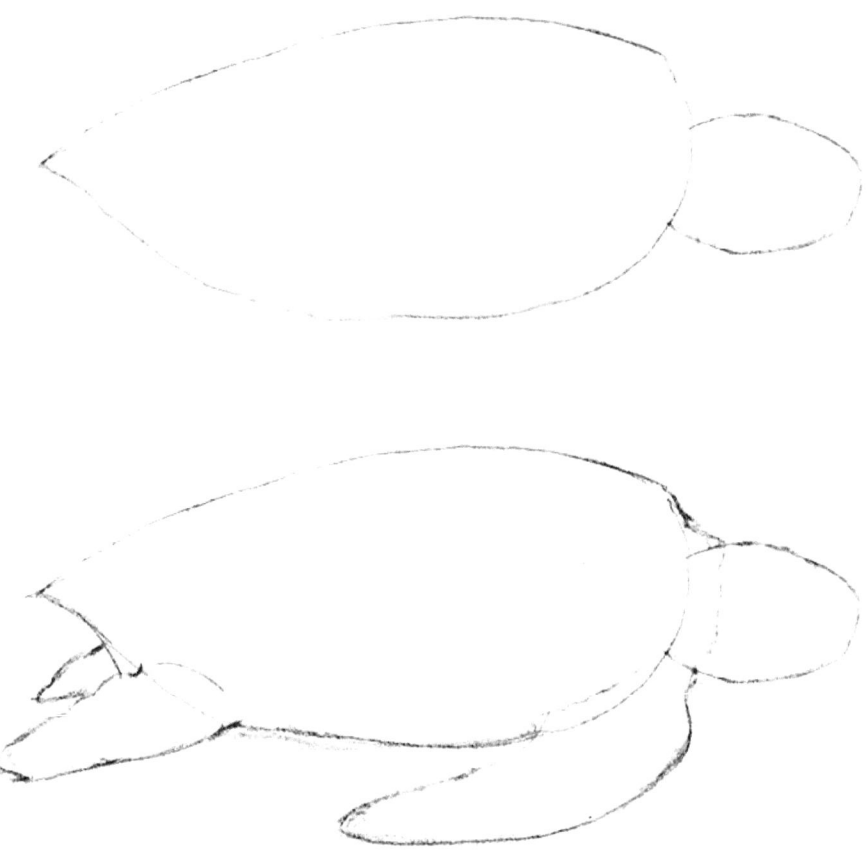

- Draw a base.

Establish the primary shape of the turtle by drawing a base. Use a shape of a teardrop or an outline silhouette of a corn. Establish the size of the head using an oblong.

- Modify the outline.

Draw main outline of the turtle's figure based on the primary shapes. The front flippers should be significantly longer and relatively wider than the flippers at the back. The nape should be covered by the shell.

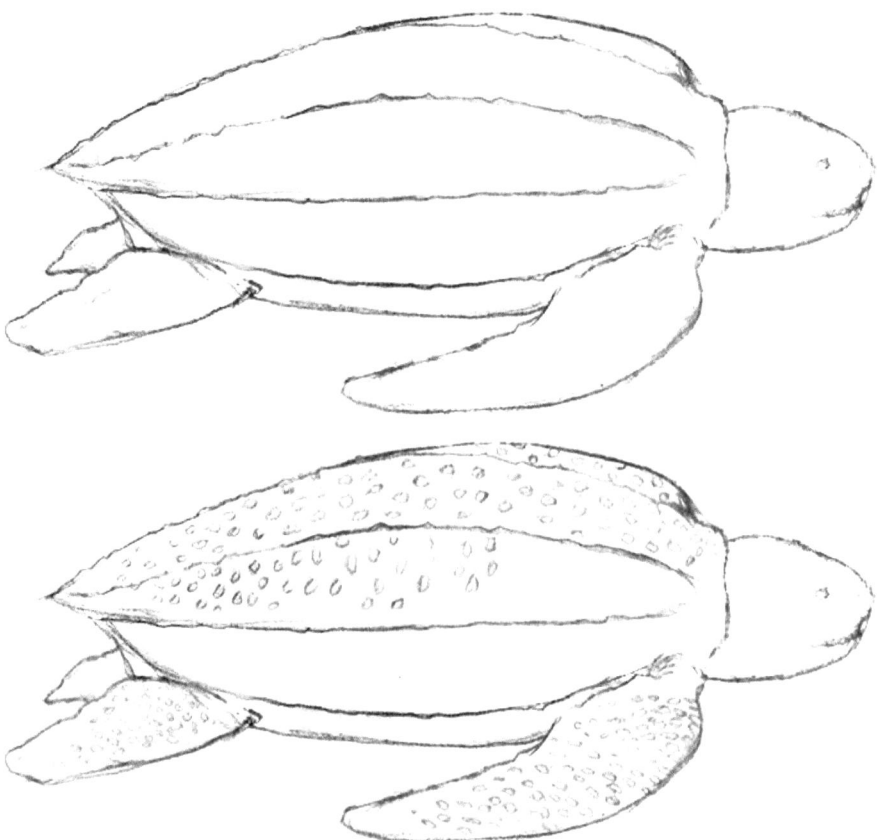

- Define the ridges of the carapace.

In this angle, only five of the seven protruding ridges of the carapace can be seen, with the fifth/farthest one being a part of main outline of the figure. Theses linings should bend or curve with the contour shape of the tear/corn-shaped carapace to properly establish dimensions. The linings are somehow toothed in a vaguely observable manner.

- Draw the spots on its body.

Establish the markings of the turtle. It is covered with white irregular spots from top to bottom.

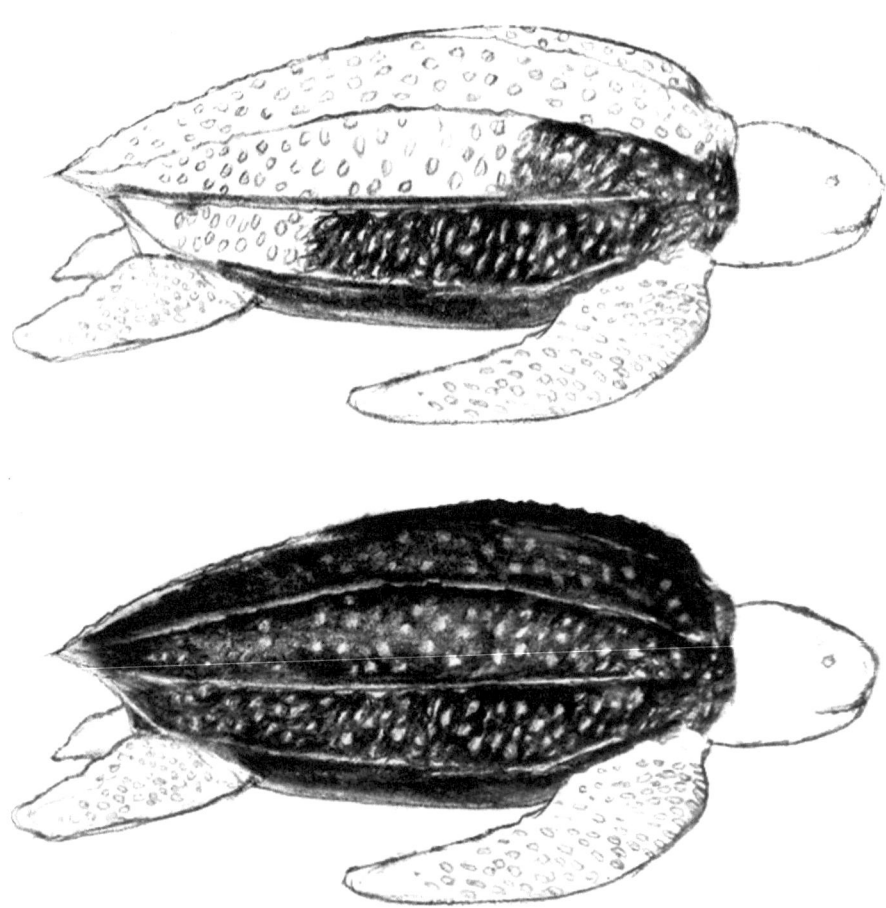

- Start shading the carapace.

The turtle is basically dark-toned, with the carapace having the same shade value as the skin (the ventral side of the turtle is much lighter but it cannot be seen in this angle).

Shade the carapace with fairly strong hand strokes, creating a dark tone. Lighten the strokes as you get to the middle areas of each row (defined by the protruding outlines of the shell) to establish its convex plane.

- Darken the farther side of the carapace.

Convey the dimensional curves of the body by darkening the farther portions (the last row of the carapace) and the lower portions right below each protrusions. Leave a highlight on the ridges to show how it protrudes from the base.

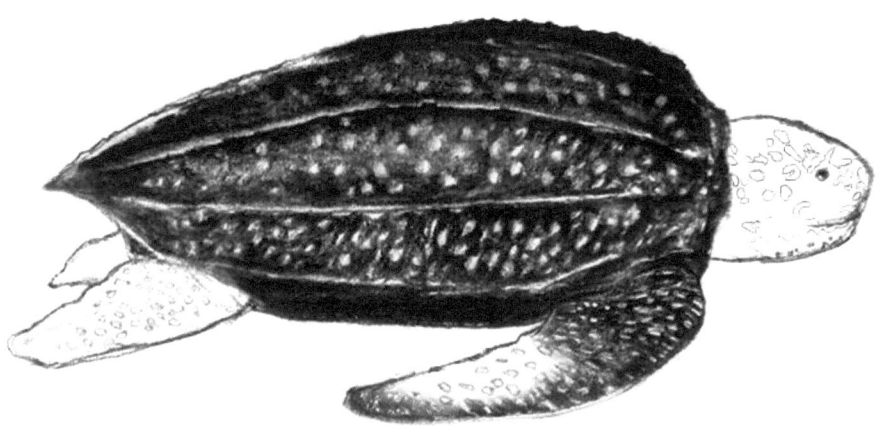

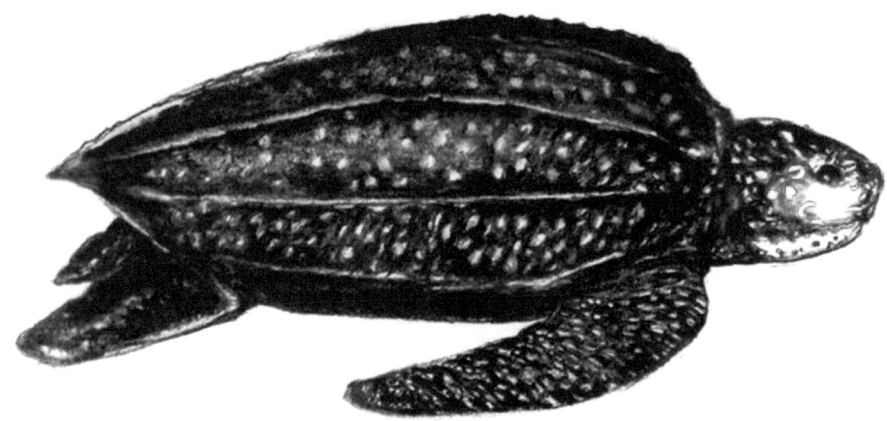

- Apply the dark value of the turtle's skin.

Apply the dark skin tone of the turtle. The dark value of the skin is just the same as the carapace. Just like how you did on the shell, avoid the spots (they should be white) as much as you can. If ever you accidently overlapped the markings, it can be retrieved with a shaved eraser or a kneaded eraser.

The dimension and angle of the flippers can also be expressed by the patterned row of spots. Although the spots should be just as random as the shell's, making few curved rows to establish the dimension of the plane (flat side of the flipper) with foreshortened spotting (spots are angled with the plane) will still make the same effect.

The bright value of the turtle's underside can only be seen to the turtle's lower jaw. Do not shade this area and just leave it with few spot marks.

- Finalize the drawing be re-darkening the darkest areas. Strengthen the dark value of the farther portions (underside of the shell, farther side of the back-flippers, overlapped areas, and subtle portions that slope inward).a strong pitch of black will complement the lighter tones and further establish the differences of the values according to the contour dimensions it should express.

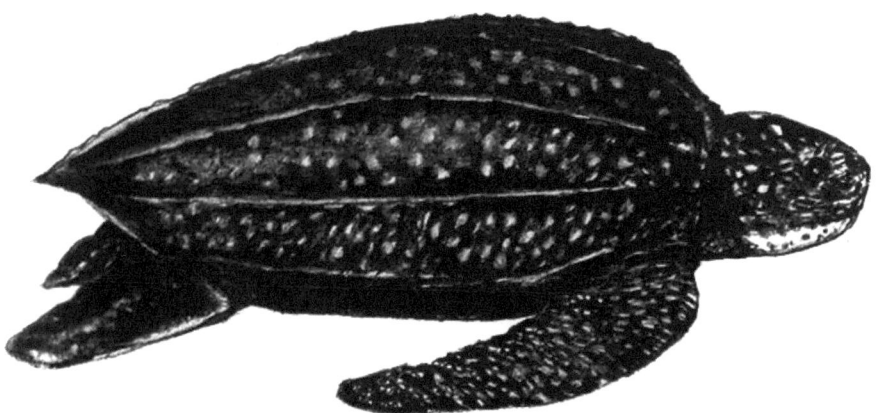

The leatherback sea turtle (also called the lute turtle, trunk turtle and leathery turtle) or Dermochelys coroacea, is the only survivor of dermochelyidae genus, a species of marine turtles that mostly existed long ago (cretaceous period). And it's sad to say that there are only few that are left of its kind. It is an active diver and rarely stays on a single place for a long time, swimming constantly to maintain a reasonably high body temperature so it could survive the cold underwater where its prey usually reside.

Softshell Turtle

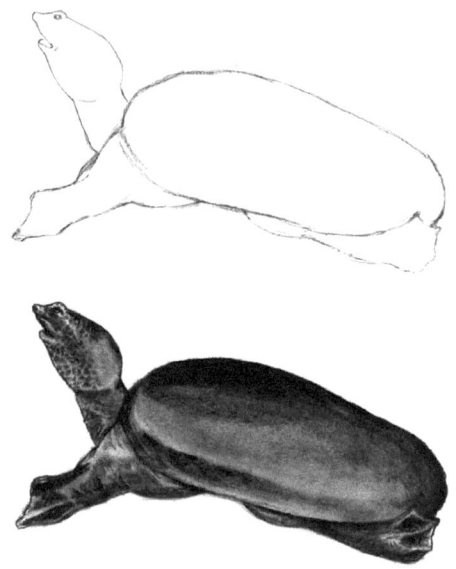

This one is recorded as the rarest of all (turtles) and is nearly extinct/critically endangered due to the loss of its natural habitat (by the means of modernization), and illegal hunting. A soft-shell turtle (as the name says) has single-formed carapace instead of the common bony shell with thick plates/scales; it is soft and not roundish dorsally; relatively flat and wide. The snout is relatively long and protruding (like a pig's).

The head of this turtle is quite big, growing a size of eight inches with a width of 4 inches. This adds up to its large and flattened carapace, to a total body length of approximately 38 to 39 inches and 28 inches in (shell) width. Softshell turtles are being hunted for their bones which are used for alternative medicines, while some local townsmen eat their meat.

The color of its body is basically mud-to-dark gray, and its thick skin is covered with faint-white speckles, mostly on the sides and rear top of its elongated head. When viewed dorsally, the shape of the shell is relatively oval, with the lower end (area of the hind limbs) more convex the upper side. The shell also contains white spotting mostly on the far edges, although it is barely noticeable. The front limb (fore fins) is somewhat wider and longer than the back limbs (hind fins). Its eyes are somewhat oddly positioned, relatively small and placed dorsally.

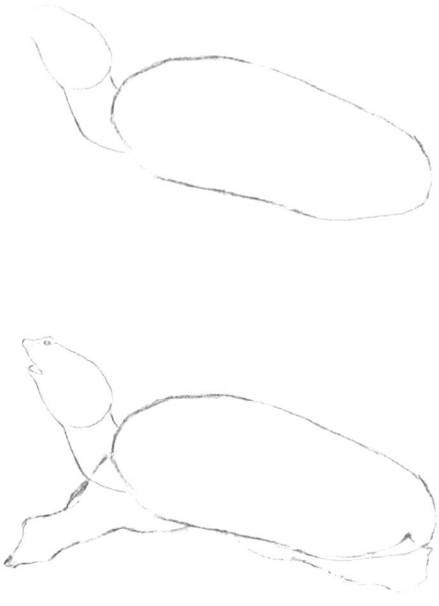

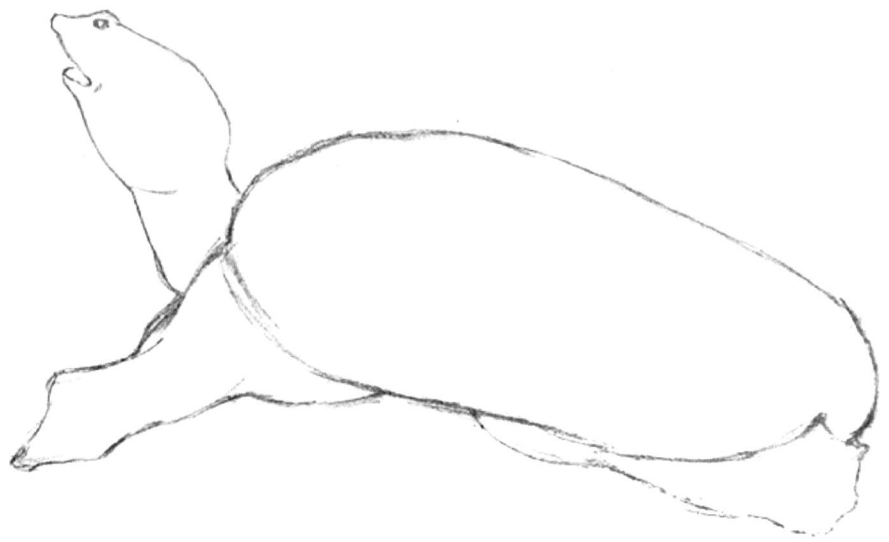

- Draw an oblong as a base.

You can use an oblong to establish the mass of the turtle's body/carapace, and another one to establish the size of the head. Connect the head to the base by drawing its neck. Adjust the shape of the base according to the angle of the turtle's figure.

- Establish the limbs/flippers.

Draw the flippers, overlap the outline of the fore limbs/front flippers should overlap the outline of the neck, and a part of the hind limb/back flippers should slightly overlap a portion of the carapace's outline.

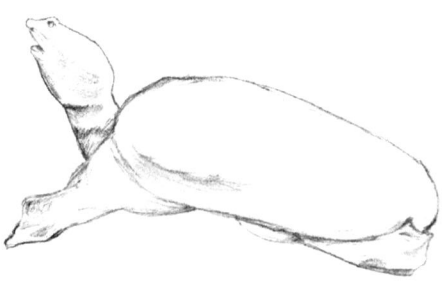

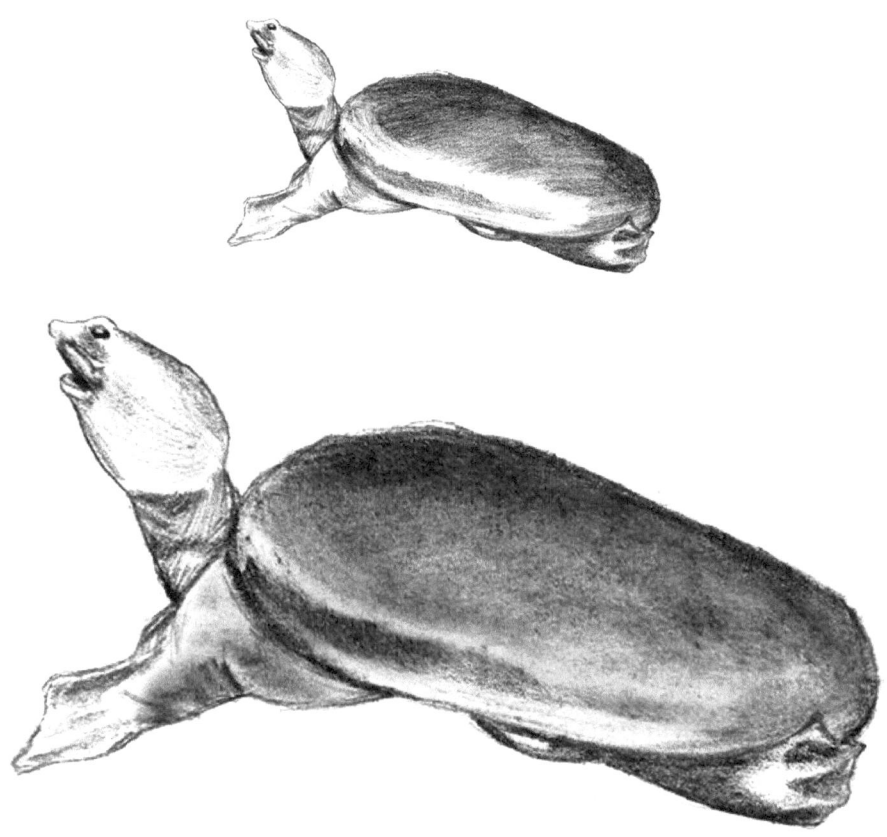

- Apply some shades to establish the planes and the curves.

Clean up the drawing by removing any unnecessary line work (sketch marks and overlapped portions). Describe the contour dimensions of the turtle by applying some shades. Use linear shading (hatches, either hatching or cross' hatching) to describe the flat and curvy planes of the figure. The side of the carapace is vaguely flat, and the top is barely bent/sloping. Establish the curve of the carapace by simply leaving a highlight. The linear shades you apply on the head should also describe its spherical form.

- Smear your shading.

Carefully distribute the shading you applied. Smear the linear shades and darken the farther sides including the subtle folds on the neck and the flippers.

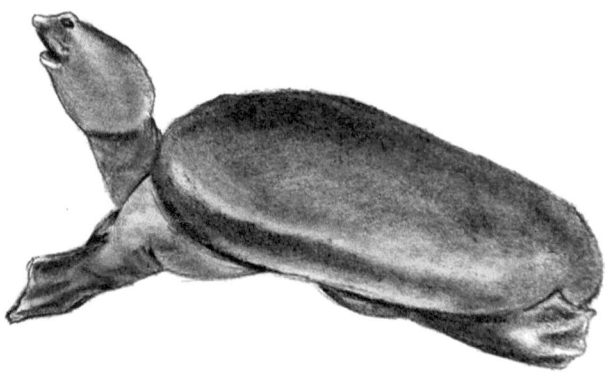

Once you are done distributing the shade tone, re-darken the areas that should appear darker.

- Again, re-darken the farther areas to further describe the contour dimensions of the turtle. The relatively flat carapace should contain a dark value on the farther side to establish its relatively flat nature.

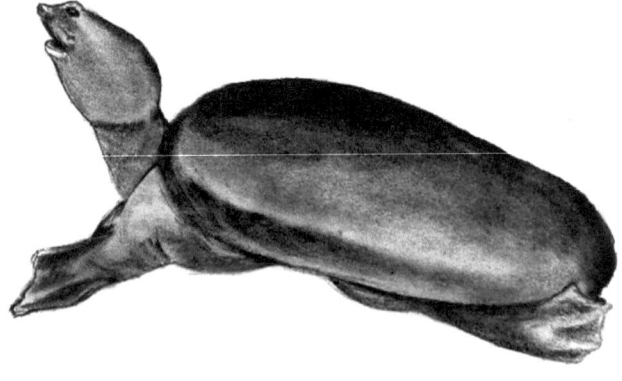

By darkening the tone, you will obtain a lighter value of gray. Shade the brighter portions (highlights on the curve of the carapace's edge and the convex of the head) into a light gray value.

- Darken the inward slopes of the ridges (under the jaw, ripples on the neck and fins).

- Define the details further.

Establish the folds and subtle crumples of the skin even further. Use short and light hatches to establish the subtle ridges of the neck and the flippers. Apply the faint patching of the skin on the turtle's head. Once you are finished, reestablish the slopes/convexity by creating faint highlights using an eraser of choice (kneaded eraser or a shaved eraser).

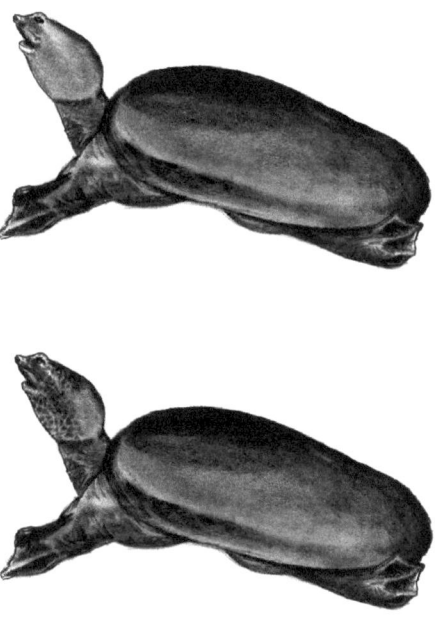

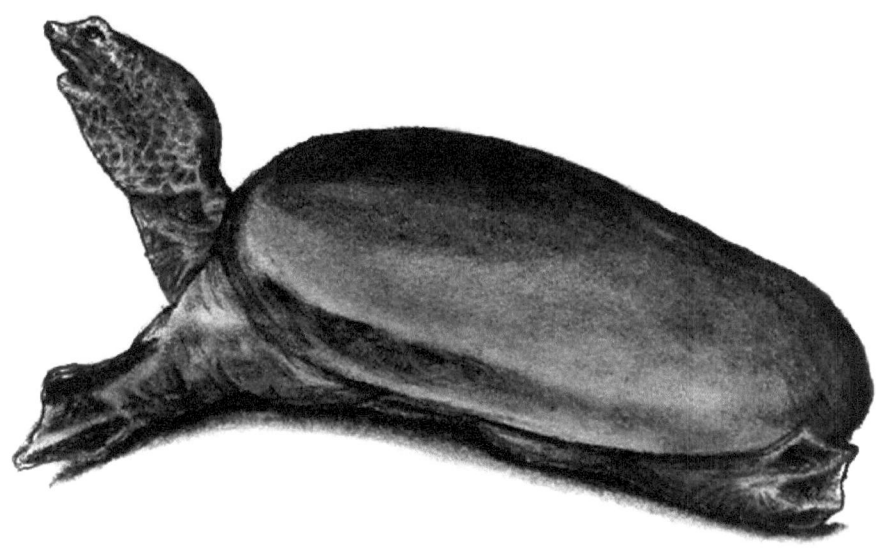

Matamata

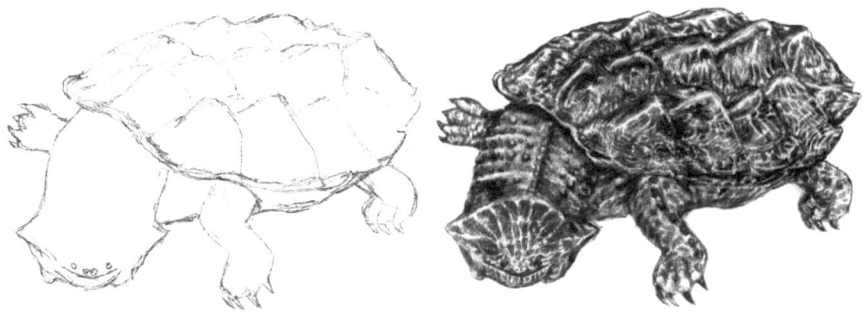

This turtle is surely the oddest-looking one amongst any other kind. The Matamata turtle, also known as Chelus fimbriata, has a number of unique physical features that makes it outstand from other turtles. Aside from having a shell with several protuberances/knobs, it also has a triangle-shaped head containing peculiar facial features.

It is known to inhabit neo-tropical locations, often seen on shallow rivers and muddy/turbid ponds or swamp pools. Matamatas are native to South America, on river basins of amazon and Orinoco River, some can be seen on the island of Trinidad, Peru and Ecuador.

The color of a Matamata turtle is basically a variation of grey, brown or green. Those with dark colors could either be greenish-brown, to grayish-brown, and the green ones are dark green or grayish green with brown tones. The brighter kinds could be yellowish brown to bright mud-brown. The color of the body is always accompanied by blotches of colors that could be the same general tone but of a different value or another color.

The dark green shell often contains blotches of reddish- brown or reddish-orange, and the mud- brown shell has dapples of a brighter brown value. The underside (of the shell, head and limbs) usually has a brighter color compared to its dorsal side/backside. Its skin is thick and rough, having ridges and protuberances surrounding the body. The neck is relatively long, containing some skin projections on both sides (left and right). Its head is wide and triangular (like a sphere head). The size of its eyes are significantly small (compared to other turtles) having only a small gap in between and located at the front edge (which is very unusual) of its arrow-shaped head. Its snout is pointed and relatively long, slightly arced upwards.

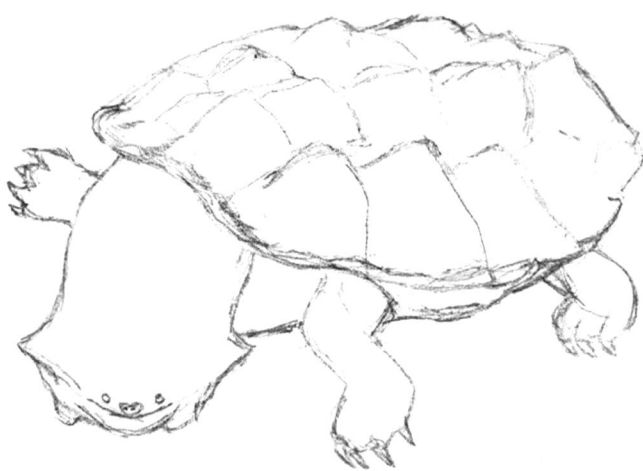

- Establish the shape of the Matamata.

The neck of the Matamata is long and relatively wide. Depending on the angle you chose, the unique triangular shape of the turtle's head should be foreshortened or modified according to its position. The outline of the carapace should describe the spiny marginal scutes, these short spikes are slightly arced upwards (slightly showing the undersides of the marginal scutes).

- Define the lumps of the carapace scute by scute.

The unique shell of this turtle is very lumpy, this feature characteristic can be established by using different values of shades.

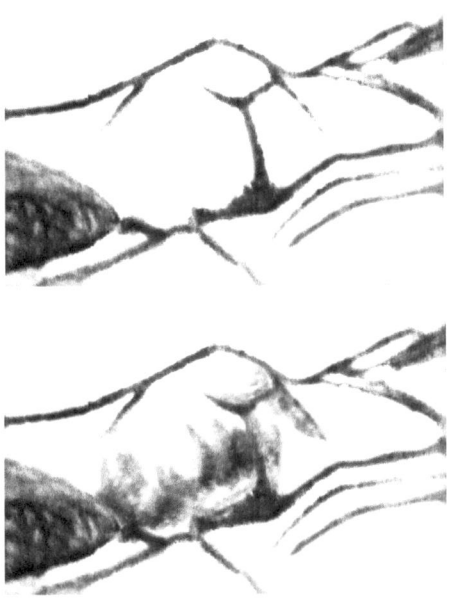

Do not use hatching or any linear shading to establish the shades, each tone value of gray should be conveyed with subtle strokes without a definite linear marking (like small and light scumbling strokes in which you will not even see the subtle spaces of each scribble). This can be easily done by carefully making numerous patch marks or markings that are used to convey the subtle protuberances of a rough plane. Using the mid-gray tone as the value to establish the color of the shell, the highlight would be the subtle slopes or protruding parts of the surface, and a darker value of gray would establish the subtle portions sloping inwards.

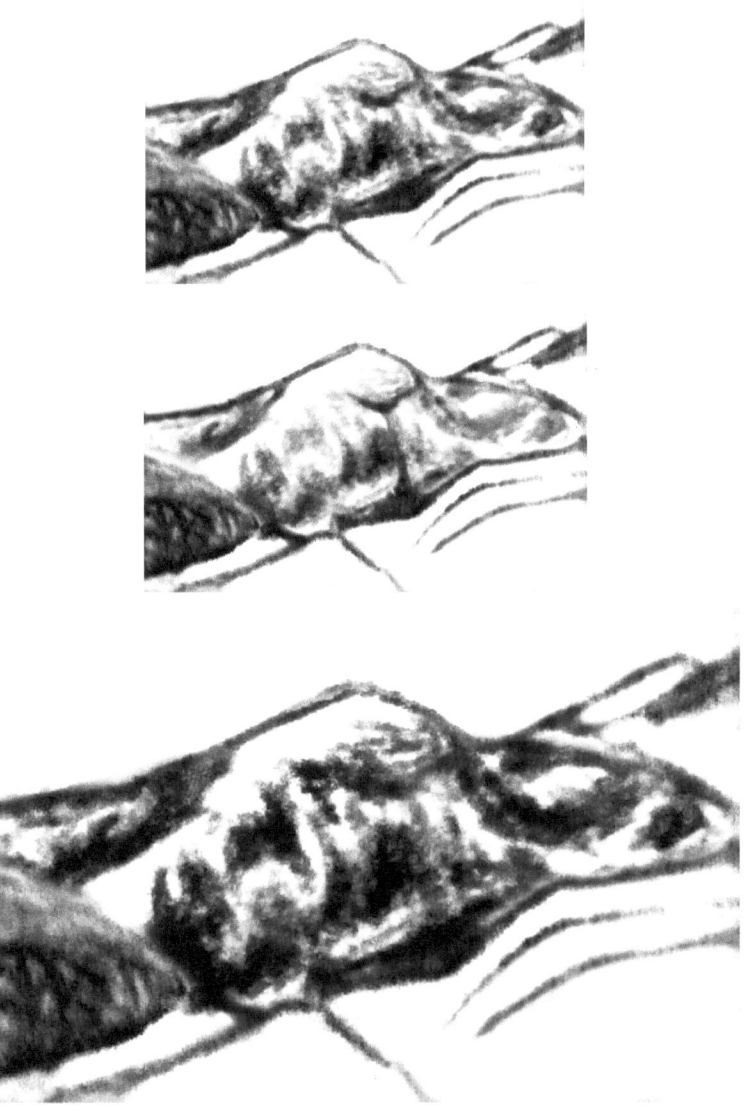

Use a fine point pencil (mechanical pencil would be easier) to establish the surface of each scute, avoid smearing the markings and try not to get too light or too dark.

- Start on the farther side of the shell.

Which scute you should start first depends on the hand you are using to draw, although it would be easier to start on the farthest row of scute so you will not smudge the shades by accident. Remember that the value of each pencil marking is important for conveying the intricate lumps of the shell effectively.

- Darken the margining outlines of the scutes.

Due to the rough knobby surface of the carapace, the sectioning of the shell might lose visual distinction. You need to keep track of the scutes' positions and how they are rowed because each scute only has one central knob and the rest of the protuberances are just like ripple marks (imagine a piece of flat clay pinched at the center).

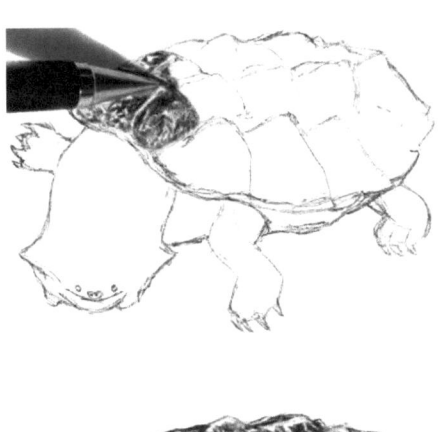

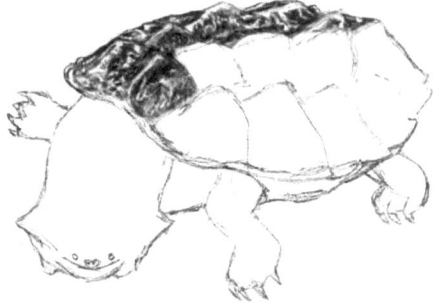

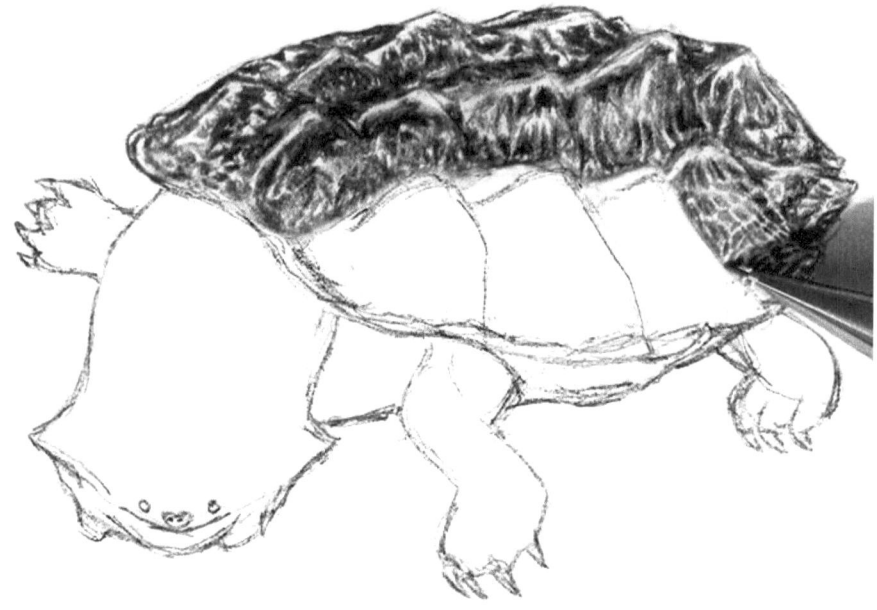

- The ridges at the inner edges (marginal scutes) appear slightly different than the ridges on the other rows.

The ripples leading to the spikes of the shell margin are like broken pieces of parallel bars decreasing in height and increasing in length as it gets to the tip (imagine cobblestones arranged to form a wavy row, or the cracks from a strong focused impact on a solid wall).

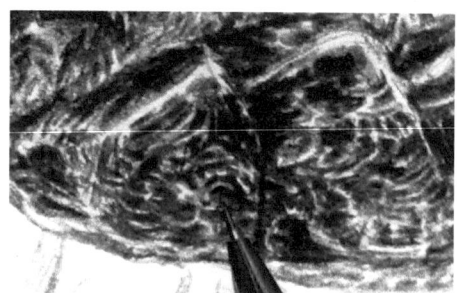

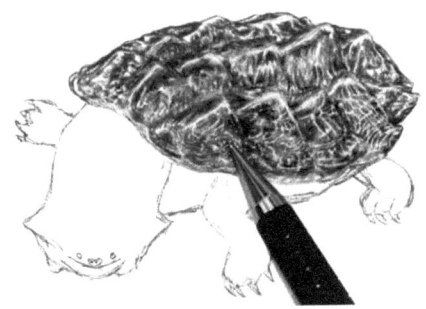

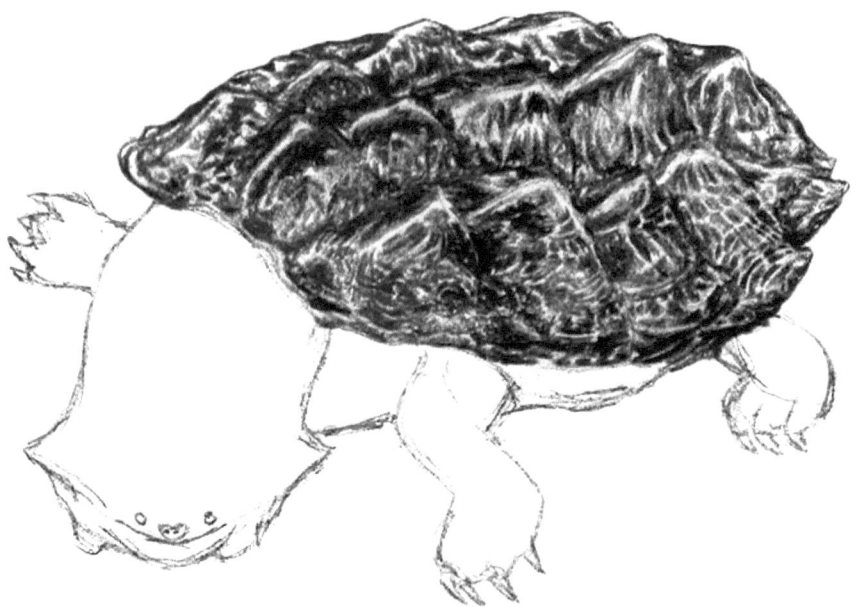

- Re-darken the farther sides and the opposing planes (area of the spikes facing the opposite side) to create a pitch (strong tones compliments the faint tones). Darken the exposed undersides of the marginal scutes and the deepest ridges sloping inwards.

- Establish the rough surface its triangular head.

The dry and thick surface of the Matamata's head also has subtle protrusions (with cracks on the skin or small warts). This detailing on the skin is hardly patterned, but the formation of the skin protrusions seems to have a certain wave or flow.

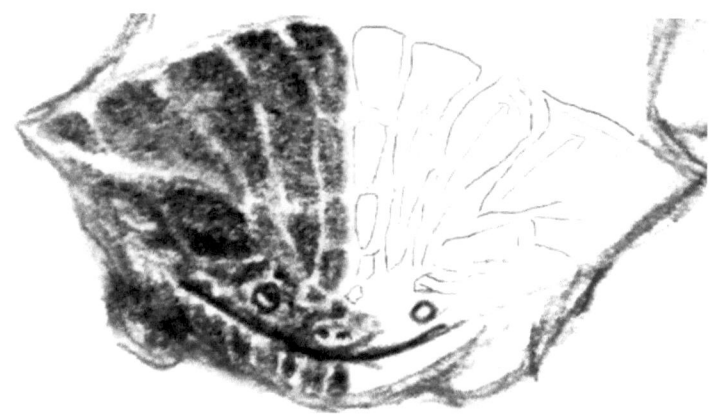

The skin patching can be conveyed with light tones of gray, make a loosely formed flow for the detailing and simply 'mirror' or copy what you are doing on one side to the other.

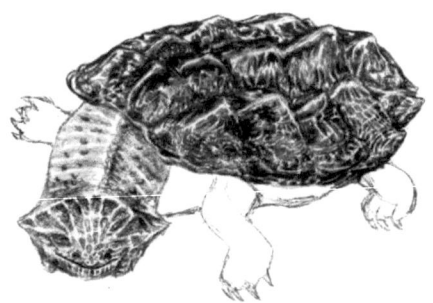

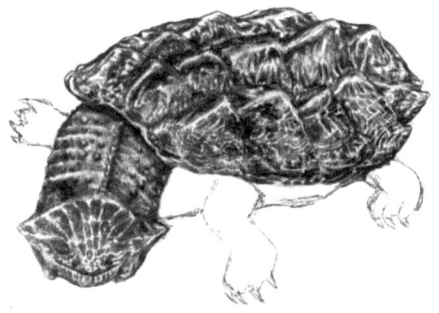

- The rough neck contains few skin protuberances/warts.

Shade the neck in a same manner you used for establishing the ridges of the head. Use the highlight to establish the subtle ripples and then apply the noticeable skin protrusions.

Darken the sides of its wide neck and add few more warts. Cast a shadow on the portion underneath the nuchal shell (area of the neck connecting to the body) and darken the inner edges of the outline.

- Define the thick and rough skin of the legs.

Define the subtle protrusions on the surface of each leg. Place a darker and thicker protuberance rowed on the margining line at the side of each leg (although this detail is not always present on Matamatas).

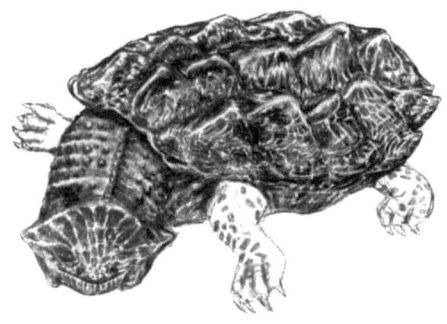

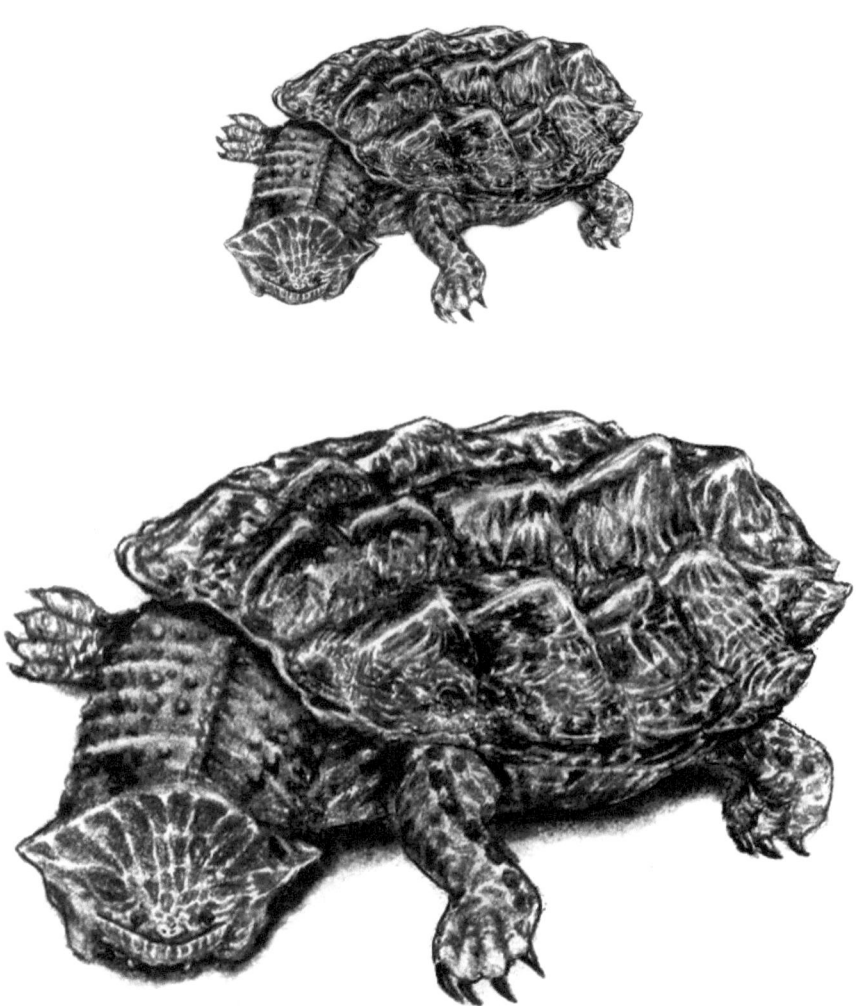

The Matamata turtle spends most of its time hidden under the surface of shallow streams but it rarely swims (it glides rather than swim, and in quite a slow manner); it simply walks the river ground with its snout sticking up above the water surface to breath. The shell of this turtle can grow a length of eighteen inches, the color of its body darkens as it matures; the dark coloration and rough texture of its skin and carapace enable it to effectively blend with its muddy habitat.

Thank you for reading.

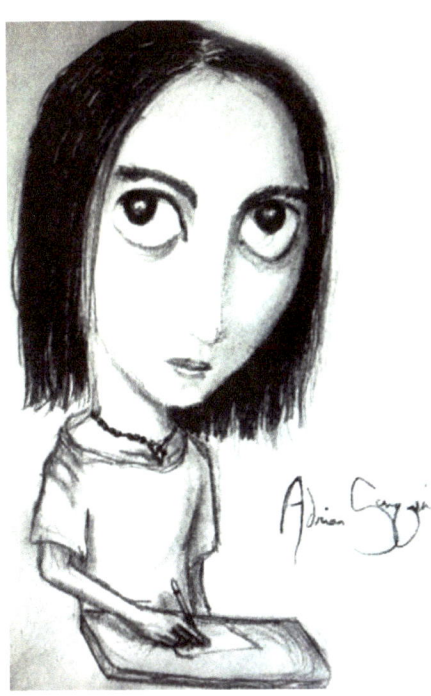

Author Bio

Adrian Sanqui

Check out some of my other books:

Manual Drawing for the Absolute Beginner

Learn to Draw People

Learn to Draw Cartoons

Learn to Draw Super Heroes

Learn to Draw Faces and Portraits

Learn to Draw Caricatures

Learn to Draw Animals in Pencil

How to Draw Lizards

Drawing Cartoon Animals for the Beginner

Drawing Insects for Beginners

Drawing Birds for Beginners

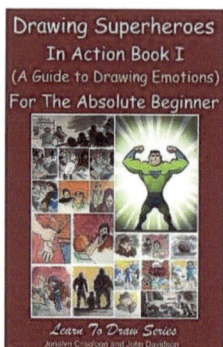

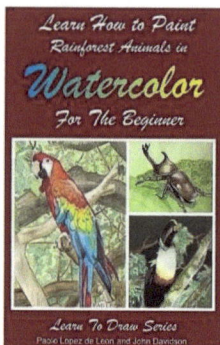

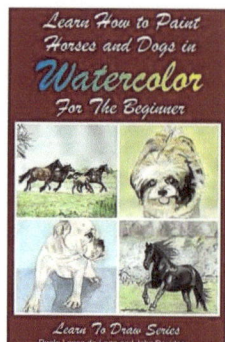

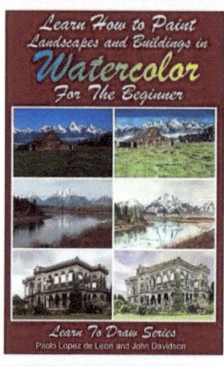

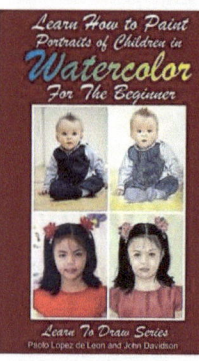

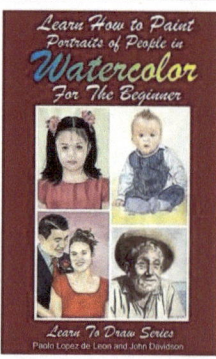

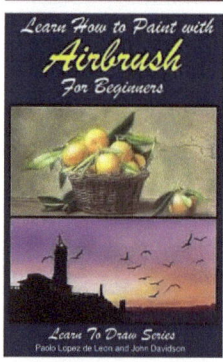

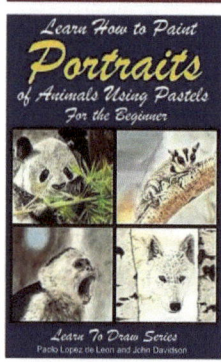

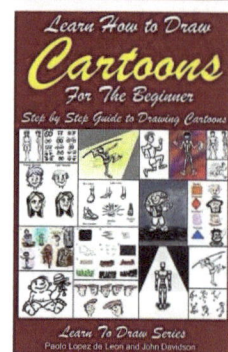

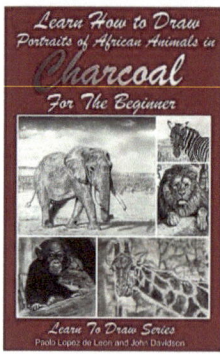

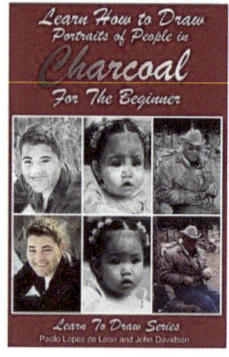

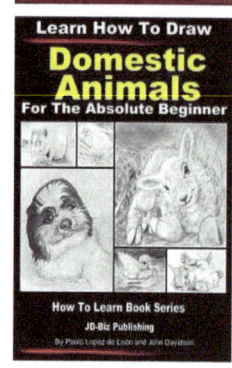

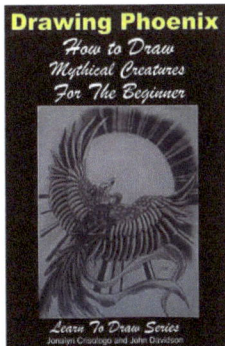

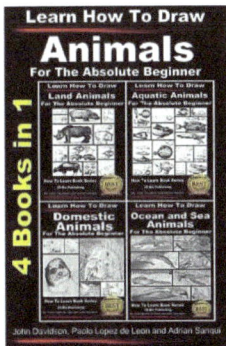

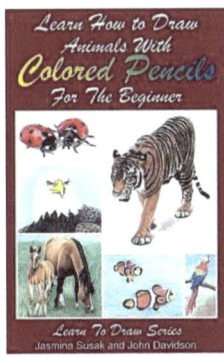

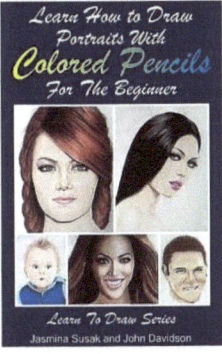

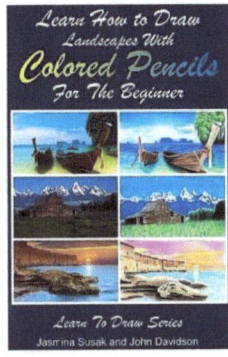

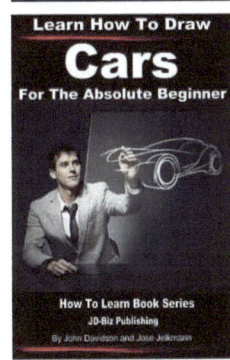

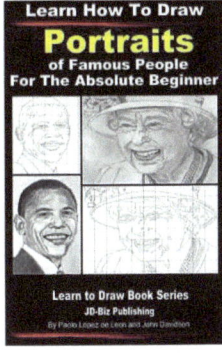

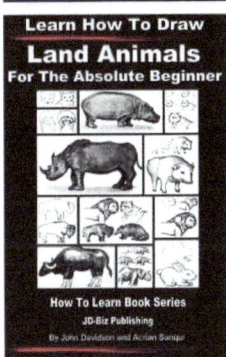

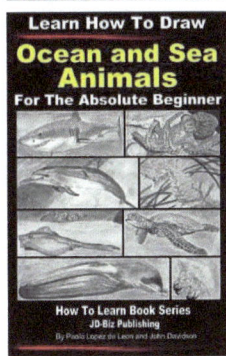

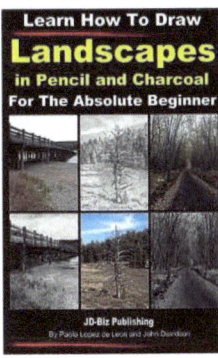

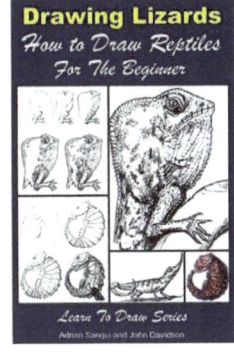

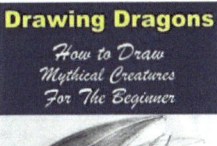

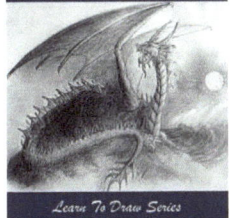

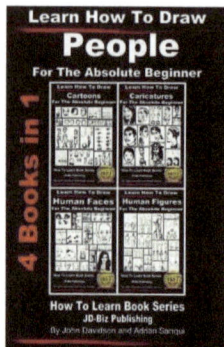

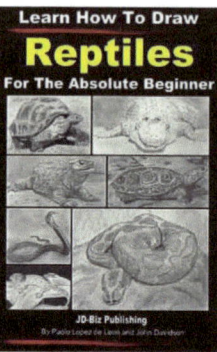

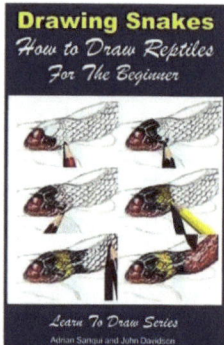

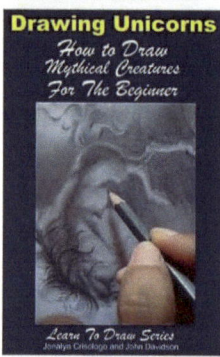

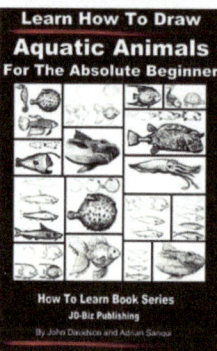

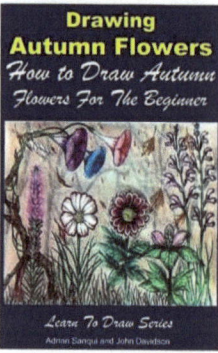

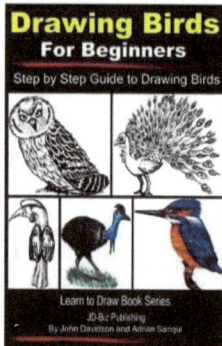

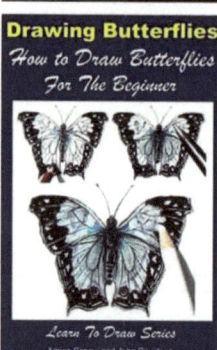

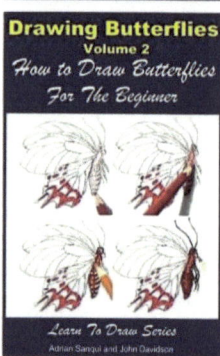

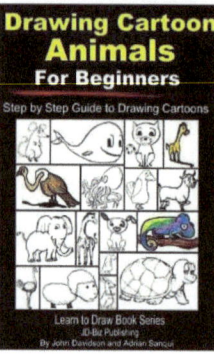

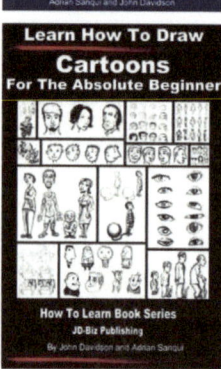

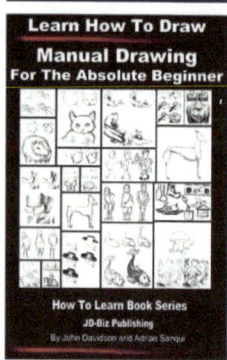

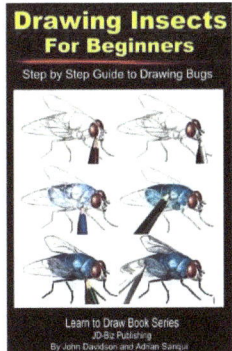

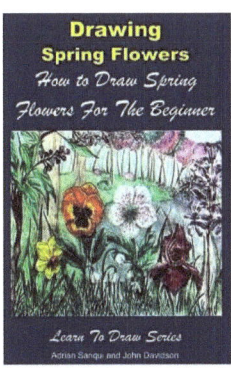

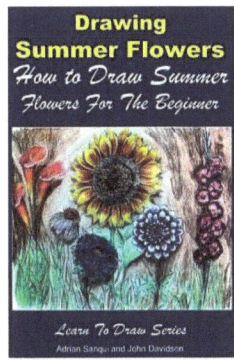

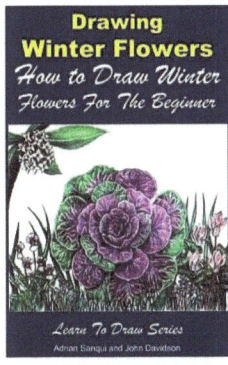

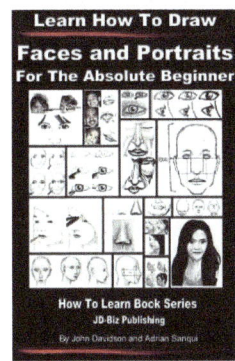

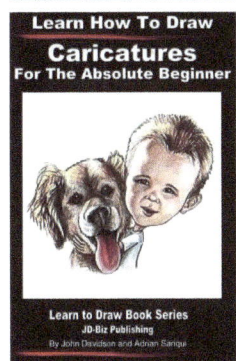

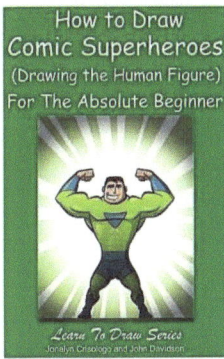

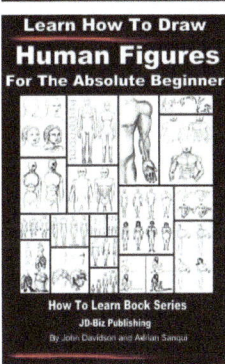

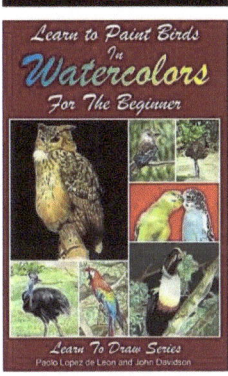

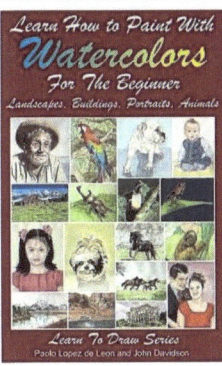

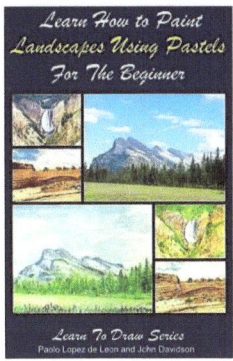

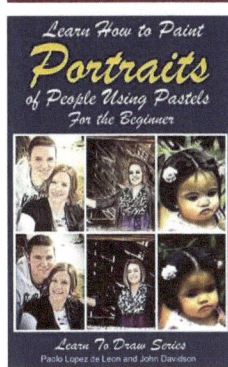

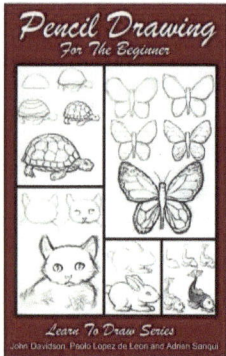

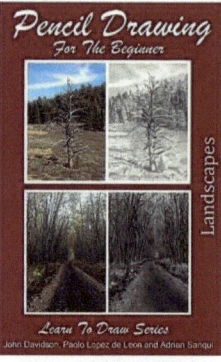

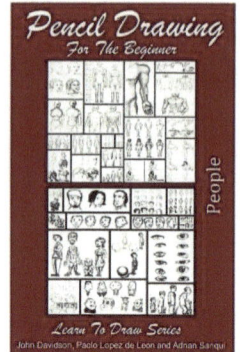

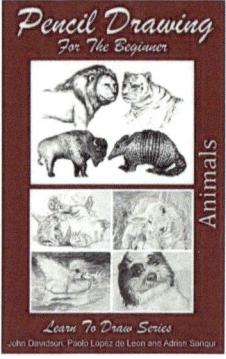

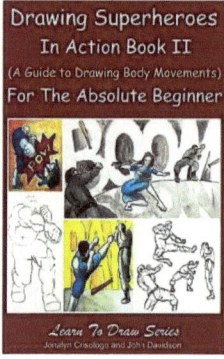

Publisher

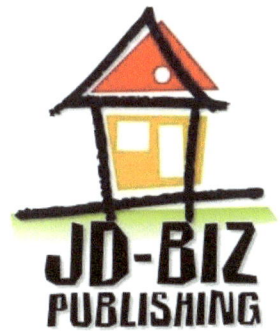

JD-Biz Corp

P O Box 374

Mendon, Utah 84325

http://www.jd-biz.com/

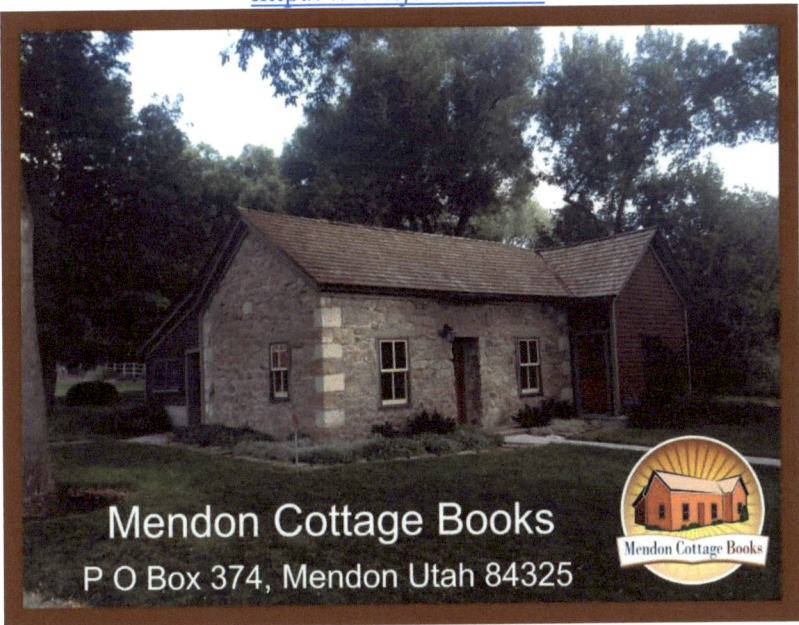

Mendon Cottage Books

P O Box 374, Mendon Utah 84325

www.ingramcontent.com/pod-product-compliance
Lightning Source LLC
Chambersburg PA
CBHW040859180526
45159CB00001B/463